SQUARE GO
by Kieran Hurley and Gary McNair

Square Go premiered in Paines Plough's Roundabout at Summerhall on 1 August 2018 as part of the Edinburgh Fringe Festival. Produced by Francesca Moody Productions in association with SEARED.

Square Go was originally commissioned and developed by Battersea Arts Centre.

CAST 2018

Max: Scott Fletche[r]
Stevie: Gavin Jon Wright

CAST 2019

Max: Scott Fletcher
Stevie: Gavin Jon Wright

CREATIVE TEAM

Direction: Finn den Hertog
Lighting: Peter Small
Original Soundtrack by Members of Frightened Rabbit
Movement: Vicki Manderson
Associate Sound: Kieran Lucas
Props and Costume: Martha Mamo
Stage Manager: Carrie Taylor

BIOGRAPHIES

KIERAN HURLEY (Playwright) is an award-winning writer, performer, theatre-maker and screenwriter whose work has been presented throughout the UK and internationally. Recent plays include *Mouthpiece* (Traverse Theatre / HighTide), *Square Go* (Francesca Moody Productions / Roundabout); *A Six-Inch Layer of Topsoil and the Fact It Rains* (Perth Theatre); *Heads Up* (Show And Tell); *Rantin* (National Theatre of Scotland). Kieran's debut screenplay *Beats*, co-written with director Brian Welsh and adapted from his hit play of the same title, is in cinemas this year executive produced by Steven Soderbergh in association with Ken Loach's Sixteen Films.

GARY MCNAIR (Playwright) is an multi award-winning writer and performer from Glasgow who aims to challenge and entertain in equal measure. Prior to *Square Go*, his last four Edinburgh Festival shows were at the Traverse theatre and all sold out: *Donald Robertson is Not a Stand Up Comedian; A Gambler's Guide To Dying; Letters To Morrissey; Locker Room Talk.* He has three times won the coveted Scotsman Fringe First Award and has toured the world with his plays. His work has been translated into multiple languages including Italian, Arabic and Japanese.

DANIEL PORTMAN (Max) Daniel originally hails from Glasgow. He is best known for playing 'Podrick Payne' in HBO's hit fantasy drama *Game of Thrones* Series 2-8 . He was nominated for an Off West End Award as 'Best Male' for his role in *The Collector*. His other credits include: Benzies in *We're Staying Right Here* at The Park Theatre, *The Collector* at Waterloo Vaults, *Black Watch* with The National Theatre of Scotland and *Philoctetes* with Oran Mor, in Glasgow. Daniels film credits include: *Angus MacDonald* in The Bruce, Frank in *The Journey*, Paul in *OutCast*.

GAVIN JON WRIGHT (Stevie) Theatre credits include work for In Motion, Perth Theatre, Citizens' Theatre, Bunbury Banter, Tron, Red Bridge Arts, Cumbernauld, National Theatre of Scotland, Vox Motus, Grid Iron, Traverse, Random Accomplice, macRobert, Pitlochry Festival Theatre and 59E59 Theaters, as well as a number of productions at Oran Mor's 'Play, Pie & A Pint'. TV credits includes *In Plain Sight, River City, Taggart, Shetland, Lip Service, Still Game* and *Dear Green Place*.

FINN DEN HERTOG (Director) Finn den Hertog is an award-winning director, writer and performer. Recent directing credits: *TBCTV: Elevenses* (Somerset House); *Square Go (Francesca Moody Productions); Playing With Books: Signs Preceding The End of The World* (Lyceum/Edinburgh Book Festival) *Misha Glenny: McMafia* (Wayward Lad); *The Men In Blue Project, Ten New Messages* (Young Vic); *Light Boxes* (Grid Iron); *Squash* (Traverse); *The Last Dictator* (Oran Mor). As associate/assistant director: *Amadeus (National Theatre) Cat On A Hot Tin Roof* (Young Vic West End); *See Me Now* (Young Vic/HighTide) *A Streetcar Named Desire (Young Vic/St Ann's Warehouse); Macbeth (Young Vic); You Once Said Yes (Look Left Look Right); The Arabian Nights* (The Tricycle). As writer: *Light Boxes*, adapted from the novel by Shane Jones. Finn has won two Scotsman Fringe First Awards - for Square Go in 2018 and for Light Boxes in 2015

PETER SMALL (Lighting) Peter Small studied Lighting Design at The Royal Academy of Dramatic Art. Since 2016 Peter has worked with Paines Plough on several projects, lighting their Growth Tour, Out of Love, Black Mountain and How To Be A Kid, all for Roundabout, their pop up touring venue. Peter has been nominated for two 2018 Off West End Best Lighting awards Black Mountain for Paines Plough at The Orange Tree Theatre and A Girl In School Uniform (Walks In To A Bar) at the New Diorama, for which he was also a finalist for the 2018 Theatre and Tech Award for Creative Innovation in Lighting. Peter has lit musical productions throughout the UK and abroad, including All Or Nothing, which toured nationally and is soon to be embarking on a run in London's West End and Tom & Jerry The Musical, staged in Egypt at the pop up EventBox Theatre, seating 3000 people. He has lit dance productions STEPLive! for the Royal Academy of Dance at the Royal Festival Hall and Sadler's Wells Theatre as well as numerous theatre productions. Other recent projects include lighting Orlando at the VAULT Festival; YOU STUPID DARKNESS! for Paines Plough at Theatre Royal Plymouth, as well asthree shows for Paines Plough's Roundabout tour 2018: How To Spot An Alien, Sticks and Stones and Island Town; Square Go for Paines Plough's Roundabout at the Edinburgh Fringe; All Or Nothing, the mod musical which transferred to the West End in 2018; Ad Libido at the Vault Festival, Edinburgh Fringe and currently touring; Out Of Love and How To Be A Kid, which toured alongside Black Mountain in the Paines Plough pop-up venue Roundabout in 2017 before transferring to the Orange Tree Theatre; Old Fools for To The Moon at the Southwark Playhouse; PLASTIC for Poleroid Theatre at the Old Red Lion and Mercury Theatre Colchester and The Rape of Lucretia for the Trinity Laban Opera.

VICKI MANDERSON (Movement) As movement director for theatre: *Moon Companion* (Coney for Natural History Museum); *ear for eye, Instructions For Correct Assembly, a profoundly affectionate, passionate devotion to someone (-noun), The Children* (Royal Court); *Br'er Cotton* (Theatre 503); *Queen Margaret, Happy Days, The Almighty Sometimes* (Royal Exchange); *Cockpit* (Lyceum Edinburgh); *We're Still Here* (NTW); *The Country Girls, Jimmy's Hall* (Abbey Dublin); *306* (NTS); *See Me Now* (Young Vic); *Details* (Grid Iron). Movement director for film: *Swirl* (Random Acts channel 4). Associate movement director for theatre includes: *Let the Right One In* (National Theatre of Scotland/Royal Court/ West End/St Ann's, New York); *In Time O' Strife, Black Watch* (National Theatre of Scotland); *The Twits* (Royal Court); *The Curious Incident of the Dog in the Night-Time* (National/West End). Vicki was nominated for best movement direction at the Irish Times Theatre awards 2018 for her work on Jimmy's Hall.

KIERAN LUCAS (Associate Sound) Theatre credits include; *Companion: Moon* and *How We Save The World* (Natural History Museum), *Orlando* (Vaults), *Mydidae* (Hope Mill Theatre), *The Ex-Boyfriend Yard Sale* (CPT/Progress Festival), *TBCTV* (Somerset House), *Gastronomic* (Norwich Theatre Royal), *Square Go* (Paines Plough Roundabout), *I Wanna Be Yours* (Paines Plough/ Tamasha UK Tour), *Plastic* (Old Red Lion), *The Ministry of Memory* (Imperial War Museum North), *The Drill* (BAC/UK Tour), *A Girl In School Uniform (Walks Into A Bar)* (New Diorama) - *Off-West End award nominated for Best Sound Design, Theatre & Technology award nominated for Best Sound Design, REMOTE* (CPT/UK Tour), *My Name Is Rachel Corrie* (Young Vic), *Hear Me Raw* (Underbelly/Arcola), *BIG GUNS* (The Yard), *I am Fortune. You Are Dark Candy* (UK Tour), *Some People Talk About Violence and NOTHING* (Summerhall/UK Tour).

Members of Frightened Rabbit (Original Soundtrack) Andy Monaghan, Simon Liddell, Billy Kennedy and Grant Hutchison are members of the Scottish indie rock band Frightened Rabbit, signed to Atlantic Records.

The producer would like to thank Thea Behbahani, Mihaela Bodlovic, Gail Carrodus, Michael Cusick, James Grieve, Hopscotch Theatre Company, Vicky Jones, Richard Lakos, Matthew Littleford, James Macnaughton, Vera Mayer, Sharon McHendry, Genevieve Moody, Giles Moody, Peter Moody, Paines Plough, George Perrin, Jonathan Salmon, Sally-Ann Salmon, Alex Waldmann, Phoebe Waller-Bridge, Michael Windsor-Ungureanu

CARRIE TAYLOR (Stage Manager) Carrie has worked as a freelance stage manager since graduating from the Royal Scottish Academy of Music and Drama in 2006. Carrie has toured Scotland extensively with companies including Scottish Opera, National Theatre of Scotland, Traverse Theatre and Catherine Wheels. Carrie has toured to New York with Hup (Starcatchers) and to 59E59 Theaters with Butterfly (Ramesh Meyyappen) as part of Brits Off Broadway 2016.

MARTHA MAMO (Props and Costume) Martha studied Stage Management at the Royal Welsh College of Music and Drama. Propping credits include: *The Court Must Have a Queen* (Hampton Court Palace), *Mixed Brain* (Paines Plough/ TiataFahodzi), *Doctor Faustus, The Alchemist, Hamlet, King Lear, The Tempest, Antony and Cleopatra* (RSC), *Valhalla* (Theatre 530), *Neighbors* (High Tide), *Realism* (Soho Theatre), *The Kreutzer Sonata* (The Gate), *A Miracle and The Pride* (Royal Court).

FRANCESCA MOODY PRODUCTIONS

Francesca Moody Productions commissions, develops and presents brave, entertaining and compelling new theatre. They work with the UK's leading playwrights and discover and nurture new talent to produce bold, award-winning shows with universal appeal and commercial potential.

The company launched in 2018 with the world premieres of ANGRY ALAN by Penelope Skinner and SQUARE GO by Kieran Hurley and Gary McNair which were both awarded a Fringe First at the Edinburgh festival before transferring to London and New York respectively.

francescamoody.com

SEARED

SEARED is the creation of actor Alex Waldmann (RSC, Globe, National Theatre, Donmar Warehouse, Almeida, Cheek by Jowl). Founded in 2010, SEARED is an independent production company dedicated to the development and facilitation if work that is provocative, politically conscious, and above all, entertaining. Previous productions include the premiere of *Years of Sunlight* by Michael McLean (Theatre 503), and sell-out revivals of *Home* by David Storey and *Brimstone & Treacle* by Dennis Potter (Arcola Theatre). Edinburgh Fringe Festival productions include the premieres of *Rose* by Hywel John, *The Ducks* by Michael McLean and *Pedestrian* by Tom Wainwright.

SQUARE GO

Kieran Hurley and Gary McNair

SQUARE GO

methuen | drama

LONDON · NEW YORK · OXFORD · NEW DELHI · SYDNEY

METHUEN DRAMA
Bloomsbury Publishing Plc
50 Bedford Square, London, WC1B 3DP, UK
1385 Broadway, New York, NY 10018, USA
29 Earlsfort Terrace, Dublin 2, Ireland

BLOOMSBURY, METHUEN DRAMA and the Methuen Drama logo
are trademarks of Bloomsbury Publishing Plc

First published in Great Britain by Oberon Books 2018
This edition published by Methuen Drama 2022

A catalogue record for this book is available from the British Library.

A catalog record for this book is available from the Library of Congress.

ISBN: PB: 978-1-3502-5879-2
ePub: 978-1-7868-2608-4

Series: Modern Plays

Printed and bound in Great Britain

To find out more about our authors and books visit www.bloomsbury.com
and sign up for our newsletters.

For Scott

You can mark our words,

you made changes to Earth

Square Go premiered in Paines Plough's Roundabout at Summerhall on 1 August 2018 as part of the Edinburgh Fringe Festival, produced by Francesca Moody Productions in association with SEARED. *Square Go* was originally commissioned and developed by Battersea Arts Centre.

CAST
Max: Scott Fletcher
Stevie: Gavin Jon Wright

CREATIVE TEAM
Director: Finn den Hertog
Producer: Francesca Moody
Lighting: Peter Small
Original Soundtrack: members of Frightened Rabbit
Movement: Vicki Manderson
Associate Sound: Kieran Lucas
Stage Manager: Carrie Taylor
Props and Costume: Martha Mamo
Associate Producer: SEARED
PR: SMP Publicity
Supported by DryWrite

Characters

MAX BROCKLEHURST
13 years old; a harmless kid, a day-dreamer.

STEVIE NIMMO
13 years old; his best mate, a loner and a bit of weirdo.

Setting

The action takes place inside the boy's toilets of
Hammerston High school; a run-of-the-mill school in a
run-of-the-mill town somewhere in Scotland, a run-of-
the-mill country.

It also sometimes takes place in the imaginations
of Max and Stevie.

It also takes place in the theatre.

A note on staging

Throughout the play, the characters talk directly
to the audience as well as to each other, with the
action moving between the scene of the school
toilets to various other locations as the boys
relay their story.

Similarly, as the story unfolds the actor playing
Stevie fleetingly embodies different characters
throughout; Danny Guthrie, Big Jordan, Max's
dad, Doctor Hobbins, and so on. This should be
indicated with a light-touch through the use of
a single prop, a discardable costume object, or
simple gesture.

At various points throughout the play, Max is
thrown into a series of live action challenges in
which he battles a character in his story, or an
inner demon. The audience is encouraged to
cheer Max on. Ideally the play should therefore
be staged in traverse or in the round, to invoke
the spirit of a live sporting event. The physical
toll of these live action challenges should be real
and increasingly visible on the actors and their
bodies throughout.

A high school boys' toilet. STEVIE NIMMO sits, alone. He is eating strawberry laces.

Suddenly the space is blasted full of booming wrestling-intro-style rock music. The space is filled with lights and smoke.

A voice is heard, offstage.

MAX: *(Offstage.)* Ladies and gentlemen, boys and girls, people of Hammerston put your hands together and show your appreciation for Hammerston High's people's champion Max Fucking Brocklehurst!

MAX appears, wearing a wrestling mask and boxing gloves. He takes big strides and works the crowd like a pro-wrestler, high-fiving the audience, climbing up on parts of the set, posing. He leads the audience in a chant.

MAX: Max! Max! Max! Max! Max!

MAX psyches himself up in the centre of the stage.

MAX: *(In voiceover.)* How To Give A Victory Speech. You've crossed the line! You've crossed the line before anyone else! Cameras surround you, there are microphones in your face, now is your time! You are a hero! Smile as much as possible, look happy! Congratulate your opponents! Say how hard they made you work, how much of a competition they made it for you. Look happy, remember to smile. Be gracious, be proud, thank the crowd, thank the fans thank your coach, thank your parents. You have defeated your opponent. You have proven your worth. You, alone, are victorious! Everybody loves you! Well done!

Suddenly the music cuts out, stark lights up. We're back in a toilet again.

STEVIE: That's shite.

MAX: What? Fuck you. You're the one that said "imagine there's a big mad crowd." Well, here's ma crowd and they fuckin love me!

STEVIE: That's pure incandescent mate. You're heavy rambunctious.

MAX: I'm just trying to get fucking – in the zone! Fucksake Stevie!

STEVIE: Just saying, as your hauners, maybe you should start by looking at the situation, as is. Instead of prancing about in the toilets like a fucking wank.

MAX: I don't want to do this Stevie, I'm just trying to get myself –

STEVIE: Shouldnae have said that thing then.

MAX: I didnae mean it.

STEVIE: Tae Danny fucking Guthrie as well, I mean / that's cosmological –

MAX: *I didnae mean it.*

STEVIE: How long have we got?

MAX: Bout an hour.

STEVIE: You need to get cracking then wee man.

MAX: "Wee man" aye?

STEVIE: Aye! Or you're gonnae get pure tabernacled. Time to start taking this fucking seriously!

MAX turns to the audience.

MAX: Okay, so I'm going to have to bring you all up to speed here. See in about one hour's time, when that clock strikes 3.35 aw this wrestling show-down stuff, will basically become, like, an actual reality. As I, Max Brocklehurst...

STEVIE: Run of the mill average naebody from class 2B.

MAX: ...step up to go toe to toe at the school gates in my very first square go. Now I understand that not all of you are from about here so yous might no really know what your square go is. Basically it's a word for like a rammy –

STEVIE: A pagger.

MAX: A heavy swedge.

STEVIE: A mano-a-mano.

MAX: A possible do-in.

STEVIE: A guaranteed pumpin, in this case.

MAX: An act of combat.

STEVIE: A bust-up.

MAX: A... fisticuffs.

STEVIE: A stramash.

MAX: A fight, basically. Man to man. A go. No weapons.
Two men, squared off against each other, toe to toe. A
square go.

STEVIE: *(Just properly understanding the phrase for the first time,
half to himself.)* Oh aye right enough –

MAX: I've dreaded hearing those words my whole life. It was
actually my dad that invented the term "square go."

STEVIE: Did he fuck! It goes back. Way back in time. First
ever square go was when Adam battered fuck ootay that
snake. Even Jesus will have had his go. It's always been
a thing. It's just the way it is. It has to happen, comes to
us all. Inevitable. A rites of passage thing.

MAX: Like your VL.

STEVIE: You're a VL.

MAX: Naw I'm no. Right, so your VL is your virgin lips.
If you've no had a kiss, you're a VL. If you're a VL,
you're a sad wee loser wi no mates. Int that right Stevie?

STEVIE: Fuck up you.

MAX: Point is, your square go is something you have to just
get done. Everyone gets their square go at some point.

STEVIE: Aye but no everybody gets their square go offay
King of the School, Neanderthal knuckle-dragger Danny
Guthrie.

MAX: Aye, alright, cheers for the reminder Stevie. Fuck.

4

STEVIE: Which is why Max here is hiding out in the bogs until the clock strikes for the end of the day. Which, you have to hand it to him, is a strategically well-chosen hiding spot if you're planning on shiting yourself.

MAX: Fuck up Stevie. You'd be shiting yourself too if Danny Guthrie was after you.

STEVIE: And just so yous all know by the way it's Danny Guthrie, alright? Never just Danny, never just Guthrie. Always Danny Guthrie. Names stick, that's just the way it is here. Like Morag Malone.

MAX: Round here Morags always get called Mo. But we already had a Mo Malone, and it wouldnae be right to have a Mo Malone and a Mo Malone 2. So everyone just calls her Macauley Culkin.

STEVIE: Here, Macauley Culkin's your brother.

MAX: Stevie, shut it. What he – when he says that right, he doesnae mean he's my brother, but… right, so, you're at school, or you're walking down the street and one of you sees a guy that just looks a wee bit suspect, like a bit of a weird guy, you know, just a guy who's a bit of a riddy, a pure beamer ay a guy right and you've got to get your pal's attention and then say "here mate, that's your brother." It sounds simple, and it is but it's an endless game.

STEVIE: It's brilliant banter.

MAX: Aye. Usually… Me and Stevie have worked out the best place for calling out a Your Brother is in Asda.

STEVIE: Nobody knows why but it is. It just is.

MAX: Stevie's got hunners ay brothers in Asda. Point is, Danny Guthrie is always Danny Guthrie and if you forget he'll break your legs.

STEVIE: Correct.

MAX: Sorry, you might no have caught our names, I'm Max.

STEVIE: Naw he's no, his real name is –

MAX: Max!

STEVIE: – Bawjaws.

MAX: Shut up Stevie! Sorry about him. Right… this is Stevie Nimmo.

STEVIE: Hiya.

MAX: Now, they say you cannae choose your family but you can choose your mates, but I'm no sure because Stevie is technically my best mate but as you can see, he is a bit of a fanny. You can tell this because of his fanny face and his fanny voice. Say something Stevie.

STEVIE: Nuh, fuck up.

MAX: Telt ye. Now, excuse me, *(To audience member.)* could you tell me something? Can you tell me what the first day of the year is?

AUDIENCE: First of January

MAX: Correct. Nobody knows why, but it is. Always has been, it's just the way things are. Now, Stevie here was born on the 26th of February, the 57th day of the year, which means that he was born eleven seventy-thirds of the way through the year.

STEVIE: What you work that oot on a... calculator?

MAX: Good one Stevie. Basically that means that he should be in the oldest fifteen percent of people born in that year. Which he probably is, but I've no proof. Although I have got proof that he's a wee knob cheese.

STEVIE: Naw ye huvnae!

MAX: Aye I huv. There's a chart and everything.

STEVIE: You're a chart.

MAX: So, the first day of the year is first of January as Stevie's brother here rightly pointed out. For some reason though, the school year doesn't start at January the first but at March the first which means that wee Stevie Nimmo here is not in the oldest fifteen percent but is now in fact the youngest person in the whole year! The runt of the litter.

STEVIE: Fuck you!

MAX: It's clearly having an adverse effect on his development. Wee, wee Stevie Nimmo. He's been told he's the youngest, and so he is the youngest.

STEVIE: At least I've got pubes.

MAX: No ye huvnae.

STEVIE: Aye I huv.

MAX: Have ye fuck? How many you got?

STEVIE: I dunno... forty-eight. Fuck you, I huv got pubes, so shut it. It's just my face.

MAX: You've just got to start shaving. Trick your face intae growing hair.

STEVIE: Is that what your maw did, aye?

MAX: Shut it Stevie, my maw shaves your maw.

STEVIE: Fuck does that work? Fucking Danny Guthrie he *needs* to shave. Guy's an ape. I heard he drinks beer out ay a glass, like to relax. Like he actually enjoys it. He's a pure corroboration, and he is one hundred percent gonnae snap your baws off.

MAX: Fucksake, whose side are you on Stevie?

STEVIE: Eh? Yours man. I'm your hauners and will have your back accordingly but I need to be realistic with the task in hand.

MAX: Aye, just my luck. Your hauners is meant tae be a hard guy that's got yer back, that can step up and kick arse for you. No offence Stevie but havin you as a hauners is like havin marshmallows fur teeth.

STEVIE: Well here I dinnae even have tae have yer back dae I, so maybe stop fucking slagging me off and calling me pubeless and that, ya fucking helmet!

MAX: Stop fucking telling me Danny Guthrie's gonnae eat me alive like it's aw just some big fucking joke, ya dick!

STEVIE: You're a dick!

MAX: You're a fucking turbo mega-dick!

STEVIE: It's like that is it? Fucking mon then, let's go!

MAX: Let's fucking go!

Lights shift to arena style lighting, wrestling music starts up, MAX hits the deck and starts doing press ups and psyching up. STEVIE addresses the audience.

STEVIE: *(To audience.)* Ok, so, this happens from time to time alright, where the two of us just wind each other up and Max gets himself all worked up and you cannae even talk to him so we just have to draw a line under it and settle it. Now, what you need to do is pick a winner and get behind them and cheer them on. Obviously I think you should be backing me, and cheering me on. Let's hear a big cheer from everyone backing me!

Audience cheer.

MAX: And let's hear a big cheer from everyone backing me!

Audience cheer.

MAX: Is that it? I said let's hear you, come on!

Audience cheer.

MAX: Let's fucking do it then!

V/O: MAX VERSUS STEVIE NIMMO!

Their is a little apprehension before talking each others' hands.

MAX: Just fucking, hold on here – not like that, like this...

9

They take each other's hands.

STEVIE: *(Shouting at the top of his lungs, like a drummer hitting sticks together.)* One, two, three, four, I declare a thumb war!

Loud music kicks in. They thumb war. Best of three. They actively whip the audience into cheering them on as they go. Ultimately, one wins.

WINNER: Once again, I rise to the top and we prove that you are a wee fanny loser.

LOSER: I'm no a loser, stop fucking calling me that.

WINNER: Stop fucking losing then.

A moment of silence.

STEVIE: Here, who would win in a fight, right, if it was Danny Guthrie versus, like, a shark.

MAX: I dunno, fuckin… shark.

STEVIE: What if it's on land but?

MAX: Fuck up Stevie.

STEVIE: Well what if it was Danny Guthrie versus fuckin, Spiderman? I think Danny Guthrie would have him. Spiderman is only good at running away really, if you think about it and the thing about Danny Guthrie is he's bound to hunt you down eventually.

MAX: Right Stevie.

STEVIE: Who would win right, if it was Spiderman versus Dr Hobbins.

MAX: Can we talk about something else please Stevie?

STEVIE: Hobbins. Hobbins would win. He'd use Physics on him. Here, do you think Dr Hobbins has even ever had his square go? Or do you think that's against, like, the rules?

MAX: What rules?

STEVIE: Teacher rules.

MAX: What?

STEVIE: Like are teachers allowed to have a square go?

MAX: They wirnae always teachers though were they?

STEVIE: Right, so what if it was Danny Guthrie right, but versus –

MAX: Stevie, can you just fucking –

STEVIE: What?

MAX: All this "some cunt versus Danny Guthrie" shite. It's pranging me out. Cos it's no any other cunt versus Danny Guthrie, is it? It's me. It's me versus Danny Guthrie. Intit?

STEVIE: Well, aye.

MAX: So I'd rather no have to think about it, if you don't mind.

The room darkens. STEVIE becomes DANNY GUTHRIE in MAX's imagination, lit from below casting a huge shadow. MAX sits on the floor at the opposite end of the room.

DANNY G: *(Makes a growling noise.)*

MAX: Danny Guthrie. A beast. A legend. A man mountain.

DANNY G: *(Growls.)*

MAX: He probably lost his virginity when he was about ten years old for all I know. Rumour has it he gets into pubs. I heard he once glassed a guy in the face for talking about his brother.

DANNY G: *(Growls.)* Never talk about my fuckin brother.

MAX: Look at him. A monster. I'd actually rather he'd just battered me right there and then, at least it'd be over with. But that's part of it. The satisfaction of knowing that until that bell rings you're sat somewhere, quite probably shiting yourself. Well, no like actually shiting yourself, not like doing an actual shit in your trousers, no like Wee Stinky Darren. But I'll no tell you about him, it'd only break your heart…

DANNY G: You better be shiting yourself!

MAX: I don't stand a fucking chance.

The lights snap back up and STEVIE is STEVIE again.

STEVIE: What kind of thinking's that Max? Snap out ay it.

MAX: I should just fucking bolt. Do a Spiderman.

STEVIE: You cannae bolt.

MAX: I should. Skip town. Pick a place on a map, pack up all my things, disappear and never come back. Fucking hate this two-bit backwater dump anyway it's an absolute shithole. I could just live somewhere else. Troon. I could go and live in Troon. What's stopping me?

STEVIE: Here, dinnae be slagging off the town, that kinda talk is pure majestic.

MAX: *(To audience.)* Look, right, just in case it's no already clear, Stevie doesnae know what majestic means, but that doesnae stop him usin it. If he hears a word he likes he just goes "I'm havin that" and uses it wherever he thinks it sounds good. And somehow it catches on! Thanks to this wee alphabetical terrorist, there was a month last year that guys were walking about describing all the girls they fancied as "apoplectic." A whole month.

STEVIE: People say our school is shite but I think that's unfair, they're just being perpendicular. The school motto is *(Reading off his school jumper.)* "Ambulate Humilitate Vestram" which means "If you wear a vest, you will be humiliated and put in an ambulance."

MAX: Naw it doesnae, it means "Walk Your Own Path, Humbly." Which basically translates to "Know Your Role, Shut Your Hole."

STEVIE: Naw, folk fae here have done things. We've even got a Hall of Fame!

MAX: It's a Wall of Fame. A very short wall between the nurse's office and the janny's cupboard. And anyway it's just a bunch ay guys that went to college about twenty years ago, nobody famous.

STEVIE: There's famous folk fae Hammerston! We've got
All The Dougies: Dougie Donnelly, Dougie Vipond,
Dougray Scott.

MAX: They're no fae… fucking… whit… are you mental?
None ay them are fae Hammerston! And Dougray
Scott's no even a Dougie, he's a Dougray.

STEVIE: Fuck's a Dougray?

MAX: Dunno.

STEVIE: It's good, I'm having that.

MAX: Fuck. Fuck, fuck, fuck –

STEVIE: Right there's no need to spin out. I've got your
back, mind?

MAX: Fuckfuckfuckfuck –

STEVIE: Look. We just need to get practical and think
tactically. Okay? Let's look at what your options are.

MAX: I could run away.

STEVIE: Not an option. Is it?

MAX: Eh…

STEVIE: Is it?

MAX: Eh… no.

STEVIE: Correct. No it fuckin is not. You could run around.
Basically you just keep movin, make it look like you're
there for the fight. If you're being generous, you can

call it bobbin and weavin, in reality it's visibly shitin yourself. Now, it might not work and it will come with it's own slaggin, but you could keep it up until it gets broken up and at least nobody can say you didn't turn up. You might want to think about this option.

MAX: What else is there?

STEVIE: One Big Punch.

MAX: That sounds good, what's that?

STEVIE: It's a long shot is what it is. When you're getting started right, you psyche yourself right up and as soon as things kick off, you launch in with one massive punch as hard as you can right in his face. Best case scenario, it knocks him out and you look like a fucking hero. Worst case, and this is much more likely, you get your punch in, it doesn't do much and then he kicks your head in. You still get a doin but everyone sees you started strong and nobody thinks you pussied out. Honour in defeat.

MAX: Dunno man, I'd probably swing for him, miss, fall over, knock myself out on the way down and he uses my face as a trampoline and everyone still thinks I'm a weedy wee shite bag! Plus, as if I'm gonnae knock Danny Guthrie out wi one punch! I thought you said we had to get practical!

STEVIE: Right, well, then the only other option is you just man up, go toe to toe and hope to actually beat him in a proper fight.

MAX: What do you mean man up? I'm manly!

STEVIE: Mate, let's look at the stats. You're a two, three a most.

MAX: Out of what?

STEVIE: Seven.

MAX: Fuck that, how?

STEVIE: You never heard ay the seven attributes of being a man?

MAX: Aye… it was my da came up wi them!

STEVIE: Fine. What are they then?

MAX: Er… I wanna say… girth?

STEVIE: Fuckin girth, what? Right. One: virility. Max, you've never been wi a lassie. Danny Guthrie on the other hand, I heard he's got three kids. 1-0 Danny. Two: stamina.

MAX: I've got this. When Big Jordan's hunting me, I outrun him I'd say 50% of the time.

STEVIE: Aye, Big Jordan's one thing. But Danny Guthrie on the other hand, he chased those guys all the way fae here to Peebles. Max, you were sick during the cross country run at sports day.

MAX: I'd just had a big lunch.

STEVIE: 2-0 Danny Guthrie. Three: fearlessness. I'll refer you back to my last point about chasin those guys. You, Max, however, shat it watching Caspar the Friendly Ghost. 3-0 Danny Guthrie. Four. Um, four is, um:

hairiness! Right. Danny's a bear, his back is like a carpet sample, whereas you my friend have got less pubes than me and I've only got forty-eight. Five: strength. I heard Danny Guthrie pushed over Mrs McGilvery's car cause it was in his way.

MAX: Bullshit

STEVIE: Heaviest thing you've lifted is the burden of being a massive disappointment. 5-0 Danny. Six: wits

MAX: Aw, come on, I've got this. The only wits that Danny Guthrie's got is when he's walkin aboot goin "Whit? Whit? Whit?" Come on, surely, that's 5-1.

STEVIE: Naw. It was your so-called wits that landed you in this mess in the first place. Showing off in Hobbins' class. Plus there's more to wits than being a smart arse, Danny's got street smarts. He knows how to handle himself. So he gets that as well. 6-0 mate. And finally, seven: respect. Max, you're alright, but you don't affect things. Nobody really knows who you are. Danny Guthrie, but. He matters. And that, my friend, is a big fat 7-0 to Danny Guthrie.

MAX: Alright 'sake, it's no a competition.

STEVIE: It will be in about forty minutes. And it's not lookin' good for you.

MAX: Thought you were on my side. Fucksake. Thought you were my hauners.

STEVIE: I am! Just saying but. 7-0. That's corrosive.

MAX: Shut it, it's no like you've had your go yet?

STEVIE: I'm different. I'll no get ma square go. I'm a peace keeper. I'm the all seeing eye. I'm the social lubricant that keeps this playground hanging together.

MAX: You're a fanny. You live in a fantasy if you think you'll never get your square go. Nobody's above getting their go. Not you. Not anybody.

STEVIE: Oh, I live in a fantasy do I? Is that right? *Mark*?

MAX: What you calling me that for, naebody calls me that.

STEVIE: It's your name but.

MAX: My name's Max.

STEVIE: Aye but what's your real name but?

MAX: It's Max!

STEVIE: Naw it's no…

MAX: For fuck… right. Fine. *(To audience.)* My real name is Mark.

STEVIE: And…

MAX: Adrian.

STEVIE: …

MAX: Kyle… Sebastian… Brocklehurst. *(To audience.)* Now, people will take the piss oot you for having four names and a stupid sounding surname like that. And it's no nice. It can get to you. Look. *(To an audience member.)* You. What's your name?

AUDIENCE: *(For example.)* Keith.

MAX: Haaaaa Keith haaaa imagine being called Keith haaaa shite haaaaaaaa. See? rubbish intit? I mean obviously there's actually nothing really wrong with the name Keith, but then again there's nothing wrong with the name Brocklehurst is there? It's not your fault at all but that's just how it is at the end of the day intit? And so I'm sorry to have put you through that Keith cos it's really not your fault, and it's a good name Keith so I'm sorry.

STEVIE: Here, Keith. Have a strawberry lace. It's cool. We're all pals here.

MAX: Point is, it's not a nice feeling is it Keith? So early on I fixed it.

STEVIE: *(Aside to audience.)* Aye plus his dad was called Mark so we was never fuckin' havin' that.

MAX: Mark Adrian Kyle Sebastian. M, A, K, S. Maks. And names stick. So yous can all call me…

STEVIE: Baw Jaws.

MAX: Fuck! Stevie! *(To audience.)* It's Max, alright. Everyone calls me Max.

STEVIE: Everyone except Big Jordan.

STEVIE becomes BIG JORDAN. He wears a baseball cap and a boxing glove on one hand.

MAX: Aye, Big Jordan, the big gangly fucknugget. Typical hard bastard fae the year above. No a Danny Guthrie.

No a legend. Just a big lanky, vicious, bullying prick.
Every day after school he chases me, and when he
catches me he gies me a punch for everyone of my daft
names. Like this:

BIG JORDAN punches his glove for every one of MAX's names.

BIG JORDAN: Mark! Adrian! Kyle! Sebastian! Brocklehurst!

MAX: Like that.

*BIG JORDAN punches his glove for every one of MAX's names
again, harder this time.*

BIG JORDAN: Mark! Adrian! Kyle! Sebastian! Brocklehurst!

MAX: Fucking hell. Right. This is basically my end of day
routine every day on my way home. I'll show you how
it works. Big Jordan spots me, and I have to fucking peg
it. The best way to lose him is a garden run, through the
back lanes. As I stand, Big Jordan is about 10 metres
behind me. I must be, 150 metres from my house.
Which is what, ten laps of these chairs? Ten laps. As
long as I get to my door before he does, I win. Ok? I'm
gonna really need your support here, I'm gonna need
yous to cheer me on. Are you ready?

MAX turns to face BIG JORDAN.

MAX: Here Jordan! Your maw looks like Ally McCoist!

V/O: MAX VERSUS BIG JORDAN!

*Music plays. MAX and BIG JORDAN race, calling out their count
as they go. MAX continues to whip the audience up into support for
him. If MAX wins, he celebrates. But he'll probably lose, distracted*

from the task of running by continually encouraging the audience to cheer him on. If BIG JORDAN wins, he will grab MAX by the throat, pin him to the floor and punch him repeatedly.

BIG JORDAN: Mark! Adrian! Kyle! Sebastian! Brocklehurst!

BIG JORDAN becomes STEVIE again, as MAX remains on the floor.

MAX: And so it fucking goes.

STEVIE: Looks like running away's fucked as an option then mate.

The room darkens again, and once more STEVIE becomes DANNY GUTHRIE in MAX's imagination.

DANNY G: You fucking better no try to run away!

MAX: Fucksake Danny Guthrie, gies peace and get out my fucking heid!

DANNY G: Too late wee baws, I live here now!

MAX: *(To audience.)* I'll tell you something about Danny Guthrie, alright?. But promise not to let on I told you. Last year, in January and we're all just back from Christmas break. Danny Guthrie and his team are all creaming it over this guy's new bike, talking about their presents; computer games, half season tickets, tracky tops, the lot. And I hear one of his team go "What did you get for Christmas, Danny Guthrie?" And there's a pause. And Danny Guthrie just goes:

DANNY G: Nuhin.

MAX: And the rest of his squad all look at each other like that, like fuck's sake whit's Danny Guthrie on about now, is he yanking our chain? And one of them almost chuckles, and says "here come on, what did you get, tell us?" And Danny Guthrie, dead serious, goes:

DANNY G: I got nuhin.

MAX: And then silence. And I'm walking away, thinking, that's weird he doesnae want to talk about Christmas the scary bastard, probably just hates happiness the big evil cockstain. And I don't know why I do it, but I look back over my shoulder and there's Danny Guthrie. Just staring at his feet. And I swear I see something on his face that looks, just for a minute, like it might be... sadness. Actual sadness. And I stop still, staring. And then he begins to lift his giant neck, and I catch sight of myself, and I turn away and hurry along as fast as I can, and as I go and can hear him behind me:

DANNY G: Gies a shot ay your bike or I'll fucking smash ye!

MAX: And as I hurry away as fast my legs will carry me, I'm thinking to myself, about all they guys on the Wall of Fame. The guys who all went to college. And intit funny how they guys have all got parents with decent jobs, and the hardest guys at school are always the ones with, like, nothing? Guys like Danny Guthrie. What's that all about?

Lights snap up and MAX is back with STEVIE. He recedes, in worry. He sits, furrowed brow. eyes closed, muttering to himself. STEVIE watches, concerned for his mate. As MAX continues in his own wee world, STEVIE addresses the audience.

STEVIE: Here, see Max right – he's got this mad hing he
likes doing. He doesnae tell anyone, I'm the only one
that kens. It's a total upholstery. What it is, right: he
watches aw these shite videos wi mad wrestlers in them.
And when I say videos, I mean they big plastic boxes
wi tape inside them. VHS which stands for Very Heavy
Shite. There's this one that he's no showed anyone else
but he's showed me. His da taped it off the telly years
ago. It's aw wee clips of this mad wrestler called Macho
Man Randy Savage. He'd written "how to be a macho
man" up the side on a sticker in permi marker. Though
if you ask me it should be called "how to be a big mad
ped." The guy is well suspect. Anyway, his da gave
it to Max one day he was home and Max was made
up. A present fi his da. He pure studies it all the time.
Just watches and takes notes on all the things he does.
Fucking bonkers. His maw hates those videos, always
trying to get them chucked out. But Max has taped a
whole bunch of back-ups and I think his maw's just
given up. He has all these wee notes, essays really, in his
notepad like "how to do a suplex" "how to do a figure
four leg lock" "how to give a victory speech." It's heavy
bossanova. So that's Max over there watching his pure
effervescent videos right, and this is me, I'm Paedo Man
Randy Fucknuts.

*STEVIE becomes MACHO MAN. MAX sits at the other end of the
space, taking notes.*

MACHO MAN: How To Give A Victory Speech. You've
crossed the line! You've crossed the line before anyone
else! Cameras surround you, there are microphones in
your face, now is your time! You are a hero!

MACHO MAN becomes STEVIE again.

STEVIE: Honestly. And it's got other stuff in it an aw, how to arm wrestle, stuff like that. And he pure practices man. Daydreams about it. Hoping that it'll help when his moment comes and he'll have to step up. Like now, preparing for his square go with Danny Guthrie.

MAX starts making an arm wrestling gesture, daydreaming.

MAX: I'm actually really good at arm wrestling. I know you might not think it to look at me but I am. I've got the theory down. It's more about technique than strength.

STEVIE becomes MACHO MAN again.

MACHO MAN: With the right technique you too can be a champ, taking down colossal opponents in your path. Colossal opponents like Danny Guthrie. Start with the arm wrestle, Max, and work your way up. You need a sparring partner, someone to practice to with. Who's a big man out there who's gonna help this kid?

MACHO MAN selects a volunteer from the audience.

MACHO MAN: Max, meet This Guy. This Guy, meet Max. If you can beat This Guy then maybe, just maybe, you can stand a chance of surviving against Danny Guthrie.

MAX: *(To opponent.)* Now, I really have to prove to myself that I can do this. It's really important that you don't let me win. It has to be real.

MACHO MAN: Alright, enough of the talk wankshaft! We do best of three, alternating arms, keep the non-active arm raised away from the table like so.

MAX: *(To audience.)* I really need you all to get behind me. Come on. *(To opponent.)* Best of luck.

V.O: MAX VERSUS THIS GUY!

Music plays. MAX and the audience member arm wrestle. A winner is revealed. MAX either celebrates, or lies face down on his desk, despondent. MACHO MAN leads the volunteer back to their seat, and then turns into becomes DR HOBBINS.

DR HOBBINS: Max. Max. Mark Adrian Kyle Sebastian Brocklehurst. Snap out of it son.

MAX: Sorry sir. *(To audience.)* That's Dr Hobbins. Our Physics teacher. It was in his class that this whole mess began.

DR HOBBINS: Nice of you to join us young Max.

MAX: Dr Hobbins is one ay they teachers that's been in the school pretty much forever. Everyone's always taking the piss ootay Hobbins cos he's a bit weird and sort ay a funny loner and he's got a weird smell aboot him like cheese and onion crisps. No a bad smell necessarily just a funny smell, for a person. And he's always saying mad stuff like:

DR HOBBINS: It's not how hard you try that matters, it's when you get it right.

MAX: Or sometimes:

DR HOBBINS: The early bird catches the worm but the second mouse gets the cheese.

MAX: Or even he'll hit oot wi something like this:

25

DR HOBBINS: This reminds me of something Bill Shankly once said.

MAX: But the thing aboot Dr Hobbins is that he's really good! He makes it interesting. He starts each lesson with what he calls a starter for ten.

DR HOBBINS: Right class it's time for your starter for ten, you all know the rules we've got ten questions, five minutes. Are you ready, well you better be because the clock begins in three, two, one: what is the circuit symbol for a lamp?

MAX: Stuff like that. It's good actually. And he's always letting me off for being late, and for daydreaming. Like he understands. Every time I show up late he just says:

DR HOBBINS: Nice of you to join us young Max.

MAX: Or if he sees me staring into space he'll snap me out of it and say the same thing:

DR HOBBINS: Nice of you to join us young Max.

DR HOBBINS becomes STEVIE again.

MAX: I like Hobbins. If I'm honest I think he thinks I'm awright an aw.

STEVIE: Is that why you said that thing? Yesterday?

MAX: Shut it Stevie. That was a slip ay the tongue, a mistake. Right? Nobody needs to know about that...

STEVIE: But it's important... dramaturgically. So, yesterday right. We're in the classroom, in Hobbins' Physics class right. We're aw at our desks, Hobbins has got us working oot ay textbooks in silence. Max is right intay it. Aw the settings on the calculator. He loves aw that shite though he'll no admit it. I've got my calculator upside down saying "boobies" and I'm passing the time drawing pictures ay cocks.

MAX: I was stuck, I wanted help with one of the questions.

STEVIE: So he's sticks up his hand right.

MAX: I stick up my hand the whole room is silent. And I don't even think about it.

STEVIE: He does that thing.

MAX: We've all done it, haven't we?

STEVIE: He does that thing. He opens his mouth, and it just comes out.

MAX is in the classroom. He is working. He slowly raises his hand to get DR HOBBINS' attention. He says:

MAX: Dad? Aw… I mean…

STEVIE: He calls Hobbins his Da. What a riddy. Gold dust to the whole class. The sort ay thing you think you'll never live down. But you can't go back, it's out there and you're stuck just playing it again and again your mind, wishing it could be different but it'll always play out the same. It's ostentatious. So that's Max over there, I'm sat over here, and yous, aw yous are the rest ay the class right. And when Max puts his hand up and calls Hobbins his da, the whole class, that's all yous, are all gonna point and go "ha, ha" like that, right. And then

27

we're all gonna chant "Hobbins is yer da, Hobbins is yer da!" I'll kick us off but it's important you all join in. Just follow me. Ready? Here he goes.

Silence. Slowly MAX's hand goes up in the air.

MAX: Dad?

STEVIE: *(With rest of the audience.)* Ha ha! *(Gesturing for audience to join in.)* Hobbins is yer da, Hobbins is yer da!

STEVIE leads the audience in the chant. After at least four rounds of this, and only once the audience are fully singing along, music comes in over the top and takes over, with the track including a vocal line of the "Hobbins is yer da" chant. In this, STEVIE becomes BIG JORDAN.

BIG JORDAN: Brockle-Hobbins!

BIG JORDAN marches over to MAX and pins him to the ground. He leathers fuck out of him.

BIG JORDAN: Mark! Adrian! Kyle! Sebastian! Fannydick! Pishflap! Fucknugget! Arsewipe! Jizzbucket! Hobbins! Hobbins! Hobbins! Brockle! Fucking! Hobbins!

BIG JORDAN steps away and becomes STEVIE, leaving MAX lying on the floor.

STEVIE: Fuck me. Still but. That's what happens when you call a teacher "dad" know what I mean? Everyone does it. Still a total whitey when it's you but. A fucking fuselage. And for Max, it was even worse than for most. The thing about Max, is that his dad, his actual dad, well… it's complicated. See, Max's dad husnae been around since he was about six or seven. He was a big

28

boozer and Max's maw kicked him oot or something, I don't know it's no even that big a deal. Or maybe it is. I dunno. He never talks aboot it. He acts like he's no bothered. But I see it. How it gets tay him. Bet you that's why he's pure delighted that Dr. Hobbins takes a wee shine tay him, know what I mean? That's why he's always daydreaming and watchin aw those tapes ay Macho Man Randy Hingmy. He's lookin for someone tay look up to.

MAX returns to a seat in a desk, as if in DR HOBBINS' class.

STEVIE: So for Max, when he put his hand to ask that question. And he opened his mouth. And what came out was:

MAX puts his hand above his head, slowly, as before.

MAX: Dad? Aw… I mean…

STEVIE: Total. Whitey. Sair yin. Gutted.

MAX stays frozen, hand above his head, as before, gutted look on his face.

STEVIE: He pretends to everyone that is dad's a legend. "My da invented square go. My da played for Dundee United. My da served in Northern Ireland. My da won the pools twice. My da invented darts. My da's been to America. My da'd batter your da. My da's got a van with seven gears." Pish. Underneath it all but, I see it. Max wanting to outdo the bastard. Get one over him. Prove himself. Conquer him once and for all so he can just be done with the whole idea ay him forever – for his maw's sake. But also just for his own. You see, deep down he knows there's only one thing his da was *actually* good at and so he'd imagine doing it better than him. Beating him, man to man, just to show him. So see when you see him drifting off on in class, if he's no thinking about Macho Wank Sweaty Bigtits, chances are he's dreaming up stuff like this:

STEVIE becomes MAX's DAD in MAX's imagination.

MAX: Dad? Dad.

MAX'S DAD silently lays out eight pint glasses of lager.

MAX'S DAD: Hi son.

MAX: Hi dad.

MAX'S DAD: How's my wee laddie?

MAX: I'm no a wee laddie anymair dad…

MAX'S DAD: Still a VL?

MAX: Naw…

MAX'S DAD: Good man. I hear you've got your square go wi Danny Guthrie.

MAX: Aye…

MAX'S DAD: That boy drinks beer out ay a glass. You can handle your drink though son? Aye? You're no a wee laddie anymair?

MAX: …

MAX'S DAD: Well let's find oot. Four pints. First man to finish is the winner. Prove yourself, son. Ready?

MAX'S DAD lays out four pints in front of MAX and four pints in front of himself.

MAX'S DAD: These are for me. These are for you.

MAX: Thanks dad. *(To audience.)* With all yous as my witness I will fucking show this bastard! Are yous with me! Come on!

V/O: MAX VERSUS MAX'S DAD!

Music plays. MAX and his DAD do a drink challenge. This has to be real. A winner emerges. The winner celebrates, the loser slumps to defeat. By now both performers are beginning to be visibly fatigued, tipsy, tired, sweaty, a bit sick. MAX needs to pull himself together.

MAX: Fuck. Fuck, fuck, fuck. So fine, right I called Hobbins dad. It's embarrassing but you need to know about it to understand what I did next. In Hobbins' class today, I burst in late again and he's already underway with the starter for 10. And he's got this picture of Einstein up on the screen.

DR HOBBINS: Now. Look at this man. Do you recognize his face? Where have you seen his big hair before? Come on. Who is this man?

MAX: And it's just staring me in the face, what a gift. Who is this man? Look at his big weird face. You do recognize him. Look at his mad tache and his turbo bonkers hairdo. Who is he? What an opportunity! Only a day after I'd called Hobbins dad, a golden ticket, a chance to put everything right again and win the crowd back. All this firing through my mind in a split second

as I step into the classroom, see the open goal, line up
the shot and out it comes...

DR HOBBINS: Who is this man?

MAX: That's your brother!

Pause.

MAX: But there's nothing but silence. No laughter. A sharp
collective intake of breath.

DR HOBBINS: Nice of you to join us young Max, but it's
not your question yet. My question, as the rest of the
class know, was for Daniel.

MAX: Daniel? Who's Daniel.

DR HOBBINS: Are you suggesting that this is Daniel's
brother?

MAX: Daniel? Danny. No. Danny Fuckin Guthrie.

*The room darkens. STEVIE becomes DANNY GUTHRIE in MAX's
imagination. MAX hides.*

MAX: Mind I told you how you never ever spoke about
Danny Guthrie's brother?

DANNY G: What was that?

MAX: Well here's why. Danny's big brother used to be
brilliant at football and Wee Daniel – as Danny Guthrie
was known back then, simple Wee Daniel who got in
no one's way – he looked up to his brother like nothing
else. Our high school might be shite but our primary
school was mega turbo shite. Nobody ever made it from

our primary school team on to the high school team apart from Wee Daniel's big brother. And not only did he make it. He was class. A pure prospect. Top scorer two years running. Let's be honest, he was probably never gonna be captain like, he was a Guthrie after all – but fuck me did he have some clout in the school. But then overnight he goes from being this pure superstar to a nobody. Worse than that. A hate figure. He was the same guy but he was done. It was before our time but we all heard. Everyone did.

DANNY G: What you fuckin sayin?

MAX: We all heard stuff. Loads of stuff. Too much stuff for it all to be true. But it was all versions of the same. It started with him not wanting to get off way Sheila McGeechie then it was he was seen holding a guy's hand, him and some guy were getting off wi each other, him and this older guy down the pub were doing stuff in the car park, he had a thing with one of the PE teachers.

Nobody actually knows if any of it was true. Some folk say it was just the hand holding thing, but then how can you tell? Maybe they were just jealous. Because he was good at football. Or because he was, like, I dunno, comfortable. In his own skin. Like in football everyone's always touching each other, know what I mean? Hugs when you score, stuff like that. I don't know. Either way, it all took hold and it changed who he was to everyone. Well, not everyone. But enough. Enough people for it matter. That's the way it is in a town like this. Folk pounce on shit like that. That's just what happens. And labels stick.The rest of the team start saying that they don't want to share a dressing room wi him. Then everyone says he's shite at football and he does stop being good cause nobody passes to him. Team stop winning. He gets the blame. Stops getting a game. The teachers tell him it's maybe best he doesn't play for the team for a wee while he thinks about what he's doing. The fuckin teachers do that. And as for Wee Daniel, well, the playground, as we all know, can be a very cruel place.

DANNY G: Are you fucking starting like?

MAX: Wee Daniel got a right slagging for his brother, every single day. Anyone would have. "Wee Daniel your brother's a homo." "How's your poofy brother Daniel?" No half of what his brother got. But still.

And then one day his brother just dies. No one told us why, like. There was rumours. Loads of rumours but nae adults told us, so fuck knows. It's like this big mad secret. Like a riddle that we're all just meant to figure out by ourselves.

The slaggings for Wee Daniel never stopped but. Sure, it became a bigger deal but it still never stopped. Even folks' parents would be at it. Mums and dads and that. "Is that the poor wee laddie wi the bentshot brother that's deid, that's sad." And Wee Daniel just snapped. Nine years old, primary 6 but in a pure fit of rage the red mist descends and he knocks down two boys in second year of high school. Always must have had it in him but now it was out. Broke one of their ribs. Wee Daniel's brother wasn't the only one that died, that day. Wee Daniel died an aw. And the legend of the monster Danny Guthrie was born.

DANNY G: *(Growls.)*

MAX: Nobody ever told Wee Daniel, "it's wrong what you did but it's very wrong what those boys said to you." They never said, "It'll be alright, we know you're hurting." They never said "you were just sticking up for yourself, I understand." They just looked at his school prospects, looked at who his parents were, where he came from, and decided he was a monster. Danny Guthrie, the monster. And labels stick. Names stick. They decided he was a monster, so now he is

DANNY G: Fuck every one of ye! I'll show yous aw!

MAX: I want to try and explain to the class that I didn't mean it, I was just a victim of my own quick wit, it was just a game, anyone would have done it, and suddenly my brain isn't working so fast, it's just stuck on a loop of "oh fuck, oh fuck, oh fuck, oh fuck, oh fuck, oh fuck, oh fuuuuuuuuuuck." And then Danny Guthrie stands and delivers those words that I've feared for so long:

DANNY G: You. Me. Square Go.

MAX: There it is. Like a voice memo from Satan. And that's me: claimed.

The lights change back. DANNY GUTHRIE becomes STEVIE again.

STEVIE: Right Max, snap out of it you've hardly any time left.

MAX: How long we got like?

STEVIE: Couple of minutes and that's it.

MAX: Really? Right. Right, right, right. Ok, ok… fuck it,
   if I just leave now, I'll be home by the time anyone's
   looking for me.

STEVIE: No you cannae!

MAX: Look, I made a mistake. I just shouldnae have
   mentioned his brother. Right, I get it. I felt bad about
   that Stevie. Alright? I want to say I'm sorry. Can I no
   just say I'm sorry? And I should be able to say sorry!

STEVIE: But that's no how it works is it? Can you imagine
   trying to say sorry to Danny Guthrie?

MAX: Can I no just say "I get it, it's shite. It's aw shite.
   You're hurting. I hurt too. I get it man."

STEVIE: No chance! That's no how it works! That's no in the
   rules. You cannae just apologise tae Danny Guthrie –

MAX: But underneath – you have tae admit, what happened
   tae his brother –

STEVIE: What happened tae his brother was the same
   fucking thing! That guy was ground down to nothing,
   by the same fucking rules, by the same fucking thing. By
   dicks like Danny Guthrie. Every dick has got a reason
   they're a dick, doesnae change the fact that they're a
   fucking dick. I've got a handle on this place, I ken how
   it works. You step out of line, and you're punished. And
   that's how it all just carries on. And carries on. Because
   of dicks like Danny Guthrie. Why does Big Jordan need
   to knock you about every day? To impress people like
   Danny Guthrie. Why do I always make myself sick to
   get sent home before P.E? To avoid gettin humiliated off
   arseholes like Danny Guthrie, Max. Every day, you and

me and other boys like us walk into school terrified, like we cannae step out of line, because of bastards like him. And so, fuck it. Maybe you're as well daein a fucking runner after all, cos that's all we're ever daein anyway, intit?

Pause.

MAX: You really been making yourself sick before P.E. aye?

STEVIE: Dinnae act like you didnae ken. That's just felonious.

Pause.

MAX: You know what you're right, Stevie.

STEVIE: I'm always right.

MAX: You're right about aw that.

STEVIE: So you're gonnae bolt?

MAX: My da, right…

STEVIE: Aw fucksake…

MAX: Naw, listen! My da ran away from everything in his life. Right. There it is. We all know it. And if I run away now, then what? Everything continues as it is. It all just carries on, and carries on, like you just said. I walk away fae this now, what changes?

STEVIE: Nothing.

MAX: And so it's just running away, and running away forever. Naw. Fuck that, Stevie. Fuck it,

STEVIE: But what happens if you show up?

MAX shrugs.

MAX: It's drawing a line though isn't it. Stand up to the bastard.

STEVIE: Right. Fucking right!

MAX: Aye?

STEVIE: Aye! Yes! Do it!

MAX: Aye?

STEVIE: Do it tae show Big Jordan, the big gangly fucknugget!

MAX: Right! Do it tae show my Da the fucking prick!

STEVIE: Aye! Do it for Danny Guthrie's big brother! Do it for yourself!

MAX: You cannae walk away fae a go.

STEVIE: You cannot walk away fae your square go!

MAX: One way or another, this ends now!

Pause.

MAX: He's gonnae fucking kill you but.

STEVIE: I know.

The school bell goes. Pause.

MAX: Stevie can you just gie me a minute?

STEVIE: You'll show up?

MAX: Aye, aye. I'll show up. Tell him I'm coming. You're my hauners aye, you're in for me?

STEVIE: Aye, yup, I'm your hauners, I will see to it.

MAX: Just a minute. I just need a minute, that's aw.

STEVIE: Awrite, just sayin but – I'm no judging, but if you shite it that could be a heavy vocabulary –

MAX: I'm no shiting it, right, I'm just – ach fuck off and gies a minute, eh Stevie?

STEVIE: Fuck sake, I was just…

MAX: Fuck off Stevie. I'll be out in a minute!

STEVIE looks at MAX, and then leaves him. He sits in the corner and eats strawberry laces. MAX paces. STEVIE – not in the scene with MAX, but still visibly onstage - leads the audience in a chant.

STEVIE: Max! Max! Max! Max! Max!

MAX psyches himself up as the chant rises.

MAX: Let's fucking go then!

MAX disappears offstage.

V/O: MAX VERSUS DANNY GUTHRIE!

Music kicks in.

MAX: *(offstage.)* Ladies and gentleman, boys and girls, people of Hammerston put your hands together and show your appreciation for Hammerston High School's people's champion Max Fucking Brocklehurst!

MAX appears out of the music and smoke and lights, wearing a wrestling mask and boxing gloves. He takes big strides and works the crowd.

MAX: Max! Max! Max! Max! Max!

MAX psyches himself up. The music cuts out. Lights up. MAX removes his mask.

MAX: Fuck's this? Where is he? Where is everyone?

STEVIE: Nice of you to join us young Max. Dinnae worry. You're fine.

MAX: Eh?

STEVIE: You're late. As usual.

MAX: What? I'm not. I, I fucking, I was just psyching up in the bogs, I was just, naw, I'm fucking here, I'm ready to go!

STEVIE: They're aw saying you shat it.

MAX: I didnae shit it!

STEVIE: Well, that's no what they're aw saying. It's cool but. You've got away with it.

MAX: Ya wee dick, where is he? Danny Guthrie. Where the fuck is Danny fucking Guthrie!

STEVIE: He's down there. Look.

MAX: Fuck's that? Aw the chanting, and cheering?

STEVIE: That, my pubeless friends is the sound of a real square go. Danny Guthrie's fighting Big Jordan. A proper go. And stop calling me a wee dick.

MAX: What? That's my fight!

STEVIE: Naw, Max. It's Danny Guthrie's fight. Nobody cares aboot seeing you get your square go. Sure it would have been fun to see Danny kick some weedy wee cunt's cunt in but that wouldny mean nuhin. And aye, if you'd no shown up and Danny Guthrie had been left at the gates on his todd then you'd have been hunted down for being a shitebag. But fuck, now that down there Big Jordan is having his go wi Danny Guthrie. Fuck me. That matters. That's all folk care about now. Look, with any luck they'll have forgotten about you by the morning...

MAX: Naw! That's my fight!

STEVIE: Max. Let it go you daft prick! You got lucky again, you dodged a bullet. It's great you were up for standing up for yourself and everything, hang on to that. Other folk will still think you're a shitebag but that's no the point. And anyway, better to be a shitebag than a dead shitebag.

MAX: Fuck up you! I'm no a shitebag so shut your hole ya wee weasley dick!

STEVIE: Stop fucking calling me that! Awright! Wee dick. Wee weasley dick. You think that around me you're the big man, the hard man, the fucking macho man, well you're fucking no!

MAX: You're always tripping me up, making me look like a wee shitebag! I bet you did this!

STEVIE: Whit?

MAX: You probably set this up, didn't you? Make me look daft? Or cause you were scared ay having to actually be my hauners?

STEVIE: Fuck you on about?

MAX: I'm sick ay your pish Stevie!

STEVIE: I'm sick ay you!

MAX: Well fuck you!

STEVIE: Fuck you!

MAX: You, me…

STEVIE: You and fucking me!

MAX/STEVIE: Square go!

V/O: MAX VERSUS STEVIE NIMMO!

MAX and STEVIE both don wrestling masks and boxing gloves. They walk towards each other and tap gloves.

Strobe lights. Loud speed metal plays. The boys start knocking lumps out of each other. There are several rounds of this, interspersed by a bell and a break in which we return to normal lights and no music. The bouts of fighting are high energy, vitriolic, rage-fuelled. What they lack in technique they make up for in anger. In the breaks, the performers are increasingly visibly exhausted and suffering. They gasp as they try to catch their

42

breath. They lean on the wall, close to giving up. They scream at the ceiling to try to motivate themselves. They try to motivate the audience to continue to cheer them along. It becomes harder and harder to do so. As soon as a bell goes they are straight back in again, like wolves. Eventually MAX begins to get the better of STEVIE. A couple of swift blows from MAX, STEVIE howls, goes down and stays down. The music stops. MAX stands over STEVIE, lit from below, his shadow cast huge on the wall behind him, exactly like Danny Guthrie's shadow from before. MAX stands up and takes a piece of paper from his pocket. He reads from it, quiet, slow, and sad, without any sense of celebration.

MAX: How To Give A Victory Speech. You've crossed
    the line. You've crossed the line before anyone else.
    Cameras surround you, there are microphones in your
    face, now is your time. You are a hero. Smile as much
    as possible, look happy. Congratulate your opponents.
    Say how hard they made you work, how much of
    a competition they made it for you. Look happy,
    remember to smile. Be gracious, be proud, thank the
    crowd, thank the fans thank your coach, thank your
    parents. You have defeated your opponent. You have
    proven your worth. You, alone, are victorious. You're
    not shite. You're not worthless. You're not a fuckin
    naebody. Everybody loves you now. Well done.

*Long silence. STEVIE still lies on the ground and doesn't look up.
MAX drops the note to the ground. He stands, staring at the floor.*

STEVIE: *(From the ground.)* Max?

Pause.

STEVIE: *(Looks around and points to someone in the audience.)* I
    see your brother's come out to support you. That's nice.

MAX looks up.

MAX: Your brother's your da mate.

STEVIE: Your da's a jobby.

MAX: Think you're maybe right there. Still but. Your maw
smells ay Camembert. Fuckin Camembert, and Edam.
That's your maw.

*STEVIE slowly begins to pull himself into a sitting position, back
still to MAX.*

STEVIE: Fuck you, I like Edam. You ever had Edam? It's a
pure Dougray.

MAX: What you on about?

STEVIE: Edam.

*MAX, tired, slowly wanders in STEVIE's direction. They don't
look at each other.*

MAX: Fuck up Stevie. Aw you eat is strawberry laces.
You've never even heard ay Edam.

STEVIE: Aye I have. It tastes like cheese strings.

*MAX sits down next to STEVIE. They wind up sitting back to
back, leaning on each other, exhausted.*

MAX: You're a cheese string.

STEVIE: Your maw's a cheese string.

MAX: Your face is a cheese string mate.

STEVIE: Your victory speech was a pure heavy cheese string by the way. You need to stop watching they videos. They're pure wank.

MAX: Aye, maybe.

STEVIE: Still but. Macho Man's your brother.

MAX: He's your brother.

STEVIE: He's your brother's brother mate.

MAX: Your brother's the King of Asda.

STEVIE: Your maw's your brother.

MAX: Fuck you, you're a brother.

STEVIE: I'm pure you're brother mate.

MAX: You're my brother.

Pause.

MAX: Aye. Fuck.

Pause. Without looking at each other, MAX and STEVIE find themselves holding each other's hand.

STEVIE: Max?

MAX: Aye?

STEVIE: Fuck's the point eh? Fuck's the point in aw this?

MAX: I dunno.

STEVIE: Shite intit?

MAX: Aye. Aye it is.

The lights begin to fade.

STEVIE: Do you want tae just – stop it? Stop daein all this?

Pause.

MAX: Aye.

STEVIE: Fuck it. Mon. Let's go hame.

MAX: Aye. Fuck it. Let's go.

STEVIE: Aye.

MAX: Aye.

They do not move. The lights go to dark.

Blackout.